DATE DUE

GREAT BRITAIN

London

PAKISTAN

Allahabad

Ganges River

New Delhi

Amritsar

Porbandar

Sabarmati

Dandi

INDIA

PAKISTAN

Gandhi's World

1869–1948

SOUTH AFRICA

Durban

Cape Town

FOR THE ILLUMINED ONE:

He lives in wisdom who sees himself in all
and all in Him, whose love for the Lord of Love has consumed
every selfish desire and sense craving tormenting the heart.

Bhagavad-Gītā, Chapter 2, Verse 55

Margaret K. McElderry Books
An imprint of Simon & Schuster Children's Publishing Division
1230 Avenue of the Americas, New York, New York 10020

Book design by Michael Nelson
Cover and title page calligraphy by Jeanyee Wong
The text of this book was set in Calligraphic 421.
The illustrations were rendered in paint and ink.

Printed in the United States of America
2 4 6 8 10 9 7 5 3 1

Library of Congress Control Number: 00-032911

FIRST
EDITION

8-30-01

GANDHI

DEMI

Margaret K. McElderry Books

New York London Toronto Sydney Singapore

When Gandhi was thirteen years old, he was married according to Jain tradition. His wife was Kasturbai Makanji, a beautiful thirteen-year-old girl who possessed qualities of patience, strength, and courage.

Mohandas Karamchand Gandhi

was born in Porbandar, India, on October 2, 1869.
His father was a prime minister in the prince's court.
His mother was a devout woman who taught her
children about their religion, Jainism. Gandhi grew
up believing in karma—the idea that to keep a soul
clean, one should pray, be disciplined, honest, have
few possessions, and harm no one.

Gandhi was a small, shy boy, afraid of
many things, including ghosts, serpents,
and the dark. His wife laughed lovingly
at her husband, who had to sleep with
the lights on.

Gandhi felt different from other people and was a weak student. He barely graduated from high school and failed classes in college. In 1888, at his uncle's urging, Gandhi left his wife at home and went to London to study the law. For a long time he felt completely alone, a foreigner in a strange country. To make himself feel more secure, Gandhi transformed himself into an English gentleman. He lived in fancy rooms and wore fancy clothes. He learned to speak perfect English, took violin lessons, and even learned to dance the fox-trot.

But Gandhi was not happy. He felt a wide gap between his inner and outer selves and, recalling his Jain upbringing, he tried to live a simpler life. He gave up his fancy rooms, cooked his own meals, walked everywhere instead of taking public transportation, and joined the Vegetarian Society of London. His self-reliance made him much happier, although he was still awkward and shy.

Gandhi finally passed his law exams and, three years after arriving in London, he sailed back home to India.

When Gandhi got home, he learned his mother had died. Determined to succeed, Gandhi set up a law practice in Bombay. But his awkward shyness prevented him from speaking in public, and he was humiliated.

Gandhi's brother knew of a law firm in South Africa that needed a lawyer, and so, in 1893, Gandhi and his wife left India. Not only was Gandhi again a foreigner in a strange country, but he experienced racism firsthand. The color of his skin marked him for contempt and some physical abuse at the hands of white South Africans. The legal work was hard. Rather than quit the work and leave an unfriendly country, Gandhi decided to change HIMSELF so he could master any challenges.

Through his powers of self-determination and concentration, Gandhi achieved his goals and realized "the true practice of law is to find the better side of human nature and enter men's hearts." He began to look on every difficulty as an opportunity for service to others. This was to be the secret of his success for the rest of his life.

One winter night, Gandhi was traveling in the first-class section of a train on a business trip. A white male passenger insisted Gandhi sit back in third class. Gandhi refused, and a steward threw Gandhi off the train. In the cold, in the dark, in the middle of nowhere, Gandhi reflected on the deep and painful disease of prejudice.

Soon after his experience on the train, Gandhi created the theory of satyagraha, or the force of love. He wrote, "The force of love by peace always wins over violence." He determined to root out the disease of prejudice, but never to yield to violence and never to use violence against others. He vowed to bring the peace of Heaven to Earth.

At the turn of the twentieth century, South Africa was ruled by the Dutch. On August 22, 1906, the Dutch government passed the Black Act, which deprived black and Indian people of their civil rights. In response, Gandhi formed his first nonviolent mass resistance movement. Over five hundred people participated in this movement of civil disobedience.

Gandhi and his followers worked for the rights of black and Indian people. They also worked for the rights of women. Gandhi did legal work for free and helped people in desperate living conditions. He nursed sick people abandoned during a plague, bandaged lepers, and comforted the dying. "These people are my brothers and sisters," Gandhi said. "Their suffering is my suffering. The whole world is my family."

Gandhi believed deeply in the words of India's holy book, the Bhagavad-Gītā. He meditated several times a day and diminished his selfish desires by loving others and loving the "Lord of Love." He tried to avoid any angry feelings so as not to cloud his judgment. By believing in the power of love and treating everyone as his family, Gandhi discovered he was no longer shy and no longer afraid of anything.

Gandhi and his followers worked to accept the good and bad in life, to meet challenges with humility and calm, and to bring harmony to the world.

With his wife and four sons, Gandhi returned to India in 1915. As soon as he could, he began the struggle for India's independence. He wanted to rid India of its hierarchical and prejudiced caste system that placed priests at the highest social level, princes and soldiers at the next level, laborers at a third level, and the poor—the "untouchables"—at the fourth and lowest level. Gandhi called those people at the lowest level the "children of God" and was determined to liberate them.

Gandhi also worked to rid India of British oppression. For three hundred years, several thousand British people ruled over 300 million Indian people. Gandhi spoke to millions of people, asking them to practice the selfless love of satyagraha. Indians ceased to cooperate with the British and many were jailed. Many spun their own cloth so they wouldn't have to purchase British-made cloth. The white homespun cloth, called KADHI, was worn by millions of people and became the symbol of Indian independence.

The British government was furious about India's noncooperation, and in 1919, during the Amritsar massacre, British soldiers killed 379 innocent people and wounded over one thousand.

Gandhi lead a HARTAL, or nationwide strike, and the entire country of India was essentially shut down. Gandhi's nonviolent satyagraha campaign marched on, encouraged by Gandhi's words: "Nonviolence acts continuously, silently, and ceaselessly till it has transformed the diseased mass into a healthy one."

In 1922, the British imprisoned Gandhi for preaching nonviolence, defying British rule, and writing anti-British pamphlets. He was in prison for two years, but the satyagraha movement was secure.

British imperialism in India was threatened, and Gandhi was happy. He did not consider being in jail a hardship but something of which to be proud. He felt that to suffer bravely for a higher ideal was the guiding force that would make every man and woman in India free.

In hot, tropical countries like India, salt is an essential part of everyone's diet. British law in India forbade Indians from making their own salt, forcing them to buy salt from the British.

In 1930, Gandhi led the Salt March. Accompanied by seventy-eight people, Gandhi began to walk from Sabarmati to Dandi, a town on the ocean over 200 miles away. By the time Gandhi reached Dandi and picked up a pinch of sea salt in symbolic defiance of British rule, he had been joined by hundreds of thousands of people. The British government was forced to acknowledge that it was beginning to lose its stronghold on India.

After leading the Salt March and other such defiant acts, Gandhi felt the imperial British chains weakening from around the Indian people and there was much rejoicing. Gandhi's followers named him "Mahatma," which means "great soul."

The British government did not give up
their hold on India easily, however, and
Gandhi was imprisoned after his Salt
March. To put more pressure on the
British, he decided to stop eating, or to
"fast." It was a powerful and nonviolent
way of threatening the British government.
The British did not want to be responsible
for Gandhi's death, so after six days the
government agreed to a pact to protect the
civil rights of the "untouchables." This
kind of social change, brought about by
peaceful means, was Gandhi's great victory.

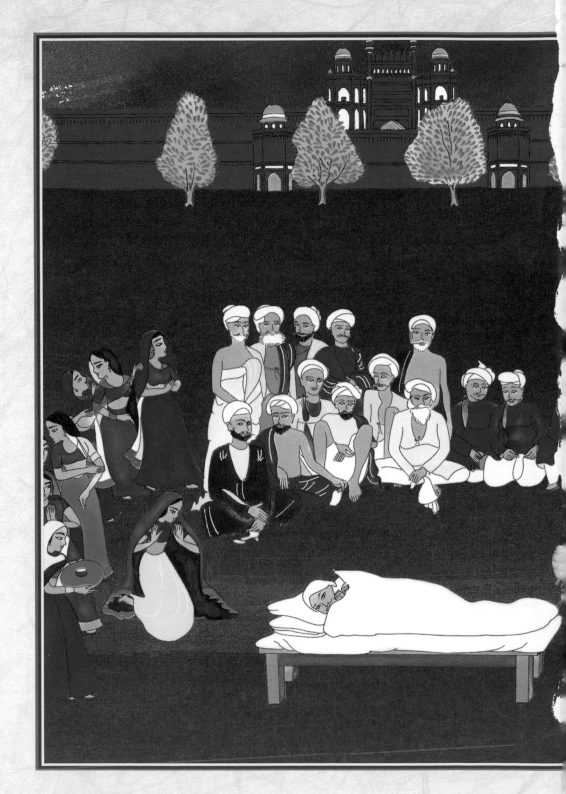

In 1944, Gandhi's wife died. Not only had she been a steadfast supporter of her husband, but she was his beloved soul mate. Gandhi mourned her loss deeply.

During World War II, Indians of Hindu
faith and Indians of Muslim faith began to
fight a civil war over differences of culture
and religion. Massacres, bloodshed, and
destruction tore at the countryside. During
this time of great chaos and suffering,
Gandhi walked barefoot through remote
ravaged villages, preaching his message of
nonviolence.

On August 12, 1947, India finally won its independence from British rule. But the country was divided into two separate countries: Hindu India to the south, led by Prime Minister Jawaharlal Nehru, and Muslim Pakistan to the north, led by President Muhammad Ali Jinnah.

Gandhi did not celebrate India's independence. He went on a fast to remind Hindus and Muslims of the importance of showing patience, understanding, and forgiveness in the face of opposition. He yearned for his people to overcome hatred with love.

Just as the satyagraha movement enabled India to overcome British rule, Gandhi trusted the movement would unify the factions that now divided India. But such unification was not to be.

The seventy-eight-year-old Gandhi almost died during his fast. He was weak, but he continued to speak to his followers.

Because Gandhi taught and expressed the brotherhood of people of all religions, he was hated by those Hindus and Muslims who believed their own religion was the only true religion.

On the evening of January 30, 1948, as Gandhi walked to a prayer meeting where thousands of people awaited him, a Hindu man named Nathuram Godse fired a gun at his heart. Gandhi fell. His last words were those of compassion and love: "RAMA, RAMA, RAMA." ("I forgive you, I love you, I bless you.")

Mahatma Gandhi was cremated in New Delhi. Millions of people in India and around the world grieved for this great messenger of peace.

At his death, Gandhi owned only a few possessions: two spoons, two pots, three monkeys, three books, one pocket watch, one pair of eyeglasses, one tin bowl (a souvenir from prison), one desk set, two pairs of sandals, and his KADHI.

Gandhi's ashes were mixed with rose petals and scattered by his family at the junction of three great Indian rivers—the Ganges, the Jumna, and the Saravati.

It is written in Gandhi's beloved Bhagavad-Gītā that "to be united with the Lord of Love . . . is the supreme state. [If one] attain[s] to this, [one will] pass from death to immortality." Mahatma Gandhi's insatiable love of humankind guided his life, changed the lives of millions, and surely made him immortal.

Author's Note

Because of his great and continual transformations, Mahatma Gandhi is one of the most extraordinary people who ever lived on Earth. From a small, shy, scared child he grew up to be a great, good, and generous man. He lived his life with the guideline that it is better to be truthful to oneself than to try to act like someone else. To be true to oneself is hard to do. Gandhi was someone who completely succeeded in living his life according to the way in which he believed life should be lived—filled with spiritual awareness, love, and peace.

Gandhi was a great Indian nationalist and spiritual leader who is often called "the father of India." His spiritual beliefs stemmed from his upbringing as a believer in Jainism, "the religion of the conquerors." Jainists believe in the eternal universe and in the brilliant human soul, which can stay pure only through prayer, discipline, honesty, and nonviolence. The symbol of Jainism is the broom that is used to sweep ants and insects away so they will not be walked upon.

Gandhi's earliest favorite book was the Bhagavad-Gītā, India's holy book on the Lord Krishna's teachings of nonpossession, equality, and self-transformation. His favorite books in the English language were Leo Tolstoy's THE KINGDOM OF GOD IS WITHIN YOU, Henry David Thoreau's ON THE DUTY OF CIVIL DISOBEDIENCE, and John Ruskin's book about living a life of good work, UNTO THIS LAST. The three books he kept with him throughout his life were the Bhagavad-Gītā, the Koran (a book sacred to people of Muslim faith), and the Bible.

Best known for the way in which he conducted his nonviolent meetings of civil disobedience, Gandhi wrote in his autobiography, THE STORY OF MY EXPERIMENTS WITH TRUTH, that "disobedience to be civil must be sincere, respectful, restrained, never defiant . . . and above all must have no ill will or hatred in it." Gandhi was against any and all forms of warfare: "If you want to see the brave, look at those who can forgive. If you want to see the heroic, look at those who can love in return for hatred."

Gandhi was greatly admired by world leaders and people from many nations. After Gandhi's assassination, the brilliant German-born American physicist Albert Einstein said of him: "Generations to come, it may be, will scarce believe that such a one as this ever in flesh and blood walked upon the earth."

It is my own great hope that we will all try to live our lives in Gandhi's honor—in truth, peace, and love.

—Demi

GREAT
BRITAIN

London

PAKISTAN

Allahabad

New Delhi

Ganges River

Amritsar

Porbandar · Sabarmati

Dandi

INDIA

PAKISTAN

Gandhi's World

1869–1948

SOUTH
AFRICA

Durban

Cape Town